# Shortchanging Girls, Shortchanging America

## Executive Summary

A nationwide poll that assesses self-esteem, educational experiences, interest in math and science, and career aspirations of girls and boys ages 9-15

Commissioned by the
American Association of University Women

Researched by Greenberg-Lake:
The Analysis Group

Published by the
American Association of University Women
1111 Sixteenth Street N.W.
Washington, DC 20036-4873
202/785-7700

First Printing: January 1991 (20,500 copies)
Second Printing: August 1994 (10,000 copies)

Cover art by Thorina Rose

**Library of Congress Cataloging-in-Publication Data**

Shortchanging Girls, Shortchanging America: executive summary: a nationwide poll that assesses self-esteem,
educational experiences, interest in math and science, and career aspirations of girls and boys ages 9–15/
commissioned by the American Association of University Women; researched by Greenberg-Lake: the Analysis Group.
2nd ed.
p. cm.

ISBN 1-879922-02-9: $8.95
1. Sex discrimination in education—United States. 2. Self-esteem in women—United States. 3. Self-esteem in
children—United States. 4. Women in mathematics—United States. 5. Women in science—United States.
6. Women—Education—United States. 7. Vocational interests—United States. 8. Educational equalization—United
States. 9. Educational surveys—United States.
I. American Association of University Women. II. Greenberg-Lake: the Analysis Group.
LC212.82.S56 1994
370.19'345--dc20                                                                                      94-27744
                                                                                                          CIP

# Shortchanging Girls, Shortchanging America

## Executive Summary

A nationwide poll that assesses self-esteem, educational experiences, interest in math and science, and career aspirations of girls and boys ages 9-15

Commissioned by the
American Association of University Women

Researched by Greenberg-Lake:
The Analysis Group

**Project advisers:**

For their invaluable work on this project, we thank:

Carol Gilligan, Harvard University; author, *In a Different Voice*; co-author, *Meeting at the Crossroads: Women's Psychology and Girls' Development*

Nancy Goldberger, psychology faculty, the Fielding Institute; co-author, *Women's Ways of Knowing: The Development of Self, Voice and Mind*

Janie Victoria Ward, assistant professor of education and human services, Simmons College

# TABLE OF CONTENTS

This is a summary of the poll that awakened the nation to the effects of gender bias in America's schools. Commissioned by the American Association of University Women and conducted by Greenberg-Lake: The Analysis Group, *Shortchanging Girls, Shortchanging America* was the first national survey to link the sharp drop in self-esteem suffered by pre-adolescent and adolescent American girls to what they learn in the classroom. Publication of the poll in 1991 shook America's consciousness and has had a far-reaching impact.

Thanks to the poll and such subsequent studies as the AAUW Educational Foundation's *The AAUW Report: How Schools Shortchange Girls*, which synthesized more than 1,300 published studies on girls in school, equity for girls has earned a firm place on the nation's education reform agenda. Educators and community leaders have discussed the problem of gender bias in open forums and are now working in communities across the nation to change the future for girls in school. Outstanding teachers have received fellowships from the AAUW Educational Foundation's Eleanor Roosevelt Fund to explore new teaching methods that bolster girls' self-confidence and enhance their learning. And in 1994 the U.S. Senate heard testimony on proposed legislation to promote equal education for girls in America's public schools.

By 1994 concern sparked by the poll and later research helped spawn a heightened sensitivity to the needs of girls. The Ms. Foundation credits AAUW, Carol Gilligan, and others for helping to inspire its national "Take Our Daughters to Work" Day. Peggy Orenstein's powerful book *Schoolgirls*, excerpted in the *New York Times Magazine* and *Glamour* magazine, grew directly out of the AAUW poll. Gender equity provisions written into "Goals 2000: Educate America," the federal education reform act passed in 1994, likewise were influenced by AAUW's seminal research.

The new awareness comes not a minute too soon. For the 23 million schoolgirls in grades K–12 of our nation's classrooms, change is clearly overdue. In an increasingly technological society, we can no longer afford to let our schools sideline girls and discourage their achievement.

For what happens to girls in school is cause for grave concern. Girls begin first grade with comparable skills and ambition to boys, but by the time girls finish high school, most have suffered a disproportionate loss of confidence in their academic abilities.

Popular culture helps deflate girls' self-esteem by marginalizing women and stereotyping their roles. Unintentionally, schools collude in the process by systematically cheating girls of classroom attention, by stressing competitive—rather than cooperative—learning, by presenting texts and lessons devoid of women as role models, and by reinforcing negative stereotypes about girls' abilities. Unconsciously, teachers and school counselors also dampen girls' aspirations, particularly in math and science.

Is it any wonder that many girls consequently become women who aim lower and achieve less than they should? Our entire society loses the contributions they might have made if only they'd been encouraged to expand their horizons. We also jeopardize girls' ability to grow into responsible citizens and parents with the skills to challenge and nurture their own children.

Changing this pattern is not just a matter of fairness but one of economic urgency. By the year 2005, women will make up 48 percent of the nation's work force. If we continue to compromise the education of half our work force, America will lose its competitive edge. The equation is that simple.

Girls' low self-esteem and consequently lower aspirations are problems that schools can—and must—help solve. And if we are to meet the pressing need for an increasingly skilled work force, we must solve the problem now. For more than a century, the American Association of University Women has worked to promote equity and education for women and girls. Today, through the energy and commitment of its 150,000 members nationwide, AAUW is working with teachers, principals, parents, and community organizations to eliminate gender bias in the classroom.

The effort began early in 1990, when AAUW commissioned an extensive examination of the comparative self-esteem levels, career aspirations, educational experiences, and math/science interests of American girls and boys. That fall the Greenberg-Lake research firm interviewed nearly 3,000 girls and boys ages 9 to 15 of varied racial and ethnic backgrounds to explore the impact of gender on their self-confidence, academic interests, and career goals. Those findings are presented in summary here.

# THE SCOPE OF THE SURVEY

■

The national self-esteem poll *Shortchanging Girls, Shortchanging America*, conducted for AAUW by Greenberg-Lake, quantifies some of the critical changes in self-perception that school experiences bring to adolescents. The survey examines the differences between girls' and boys' perceptions of themselves and their futures, and identifies critical processes at work in forming adolescents' self-esteem and identity. It then looks at the development of adolescents' aspirations and the part schools play in forming adolescents' career choices and expectations and their perceptions of gender roles. And finally, the survey examines the relationship of math and science skills to the self-esteem and career goals of the girls and boys who will make up the next century's work force.

This executive summary presents the chief survey conclusions in a highly condensed and easily accessible form. Accordingly, it often uses single dramatic responses to illustrate findings that are based on analyses of patterns across many measures. For a more complex picture and in-depth analysis, readers should consult the full 500-page survey, containing all survey questions and responses and cross-tabulations from multiple indicators, verified by the entire research team. For information, call 202/785-7761. The price for members is $60, for nonmembers $85.

Adolescence, the period of transition from childhood to adulthood, is a critical time for the development of self-identity. Dramatic changes in biology and psychology coincide with the need to make a broad set of choices and decisions. And the interpretations of gender differences that girls and boys make at this stage have a profound impact on the adult lives of women and men in our society.

*Shortchanging Girls, Shortchanging America* surveyed roughly 3,000 children— 2,374 girls and 600 boys—between grades 4 and 10 in 12 locations nationwide. The survey was conducted from Sept. 19 through Nov. 14, 1990. The sample for this study was stratified by region. Greenberg-Lake developed clusters of states and took a random selection sample across each strata and cluster proportionate to the number of school-age children in each state the previous year. Researchers analyzed survey results by gender and race—looking at responses for white girls and boys, black girls and boys, and Hispanic girls and boys—but, following standard research practice, did not report on subgroups where error was too high because of small subsample size. Topics of research and the survey language were refined in a preliminary series of focus groups.

In all, children were asked to respond to 92 questions touching on their attitudes to school, self-esteem, view of gender roles, classroom experiences, and career aspirations. Complex self-esteem measures were based on responses to a battery of 26 questions grouped into six broad categories: individual or personal self-esteem, family importance, academic confidence, isolation, voice, and social acceptance. All findings are based on multiple indicators and conclusions drawn by multiple independent analysts.

# SURVEY SUMMARY

*As girls and boys grow older, both experience a significant loss of self-esteem in a variety of areas. However, the loss is most dramatic and has the most long-lasting effect for girls. The summary presents key findings about self-esteem levels in adolescents, about the effects of young people's declining sense of self on their actions and abilities, and about institutional influences on adolescents' lives. These findings represent the beginning of an understanding of the complex relationship between adolescent self-image and careers, the differences in that relationship due to gender, and the impact of math and science on self-esteem and career aspirations.*

## A gender gap in self-esteem increases with age.

The adolescent years, marked by dramatic changes and contradictions, strongly affect the self-esteem of both girls and boys. However, the survey finds dramatic differences in levels and trends in esteem between girls and boys, with more boys than girls entering adolescence with high self-esteem and many more young men than young women leaving adolescence with high self-esteem.

Girls aged eight and nine are confident, assertive, and feel authoritative about themselves. Yet most emerge from adolescence with a poor self-image, constrained views of their future and their place in society, and

much less confidence about themselves and their abilities. Sixty percent of elementary school girls say they are "happy the way I am," a core measure of personal self-esteem. More boys, 67 percent of those surveyed, also strongly agreed with the statement.

Over the next eight years, girls' self-esteem falls 31 percentage points, with only 29 percent of high school girls describing the statement "I'm happy the way I am" as always true. Almost half of the high school boys (46 percent) retain their high self-esteem. Thus the gender gap has grown from 7 points to 17 points.

Graph A shows girls and boys experiencing a loss of self-esteem as they grow older, with adolescent girls showing a dramatically greater loss. The sharpest drops in self-esteem occur in the years between elementary school and middle school.

The drop in self-esteem during the adolescent years and the accelerating and widening gap in self-esteem between girls and boys is most clearly presented by calculating a "Self-Esteem Index" from the five tested measures of basic individual self-esteem: "I like the way I look," "I like most things about myself," "I'm happy the way I am," "Sometimes I don't like myself that much," and "I wish I were somebody else." See Graph B.

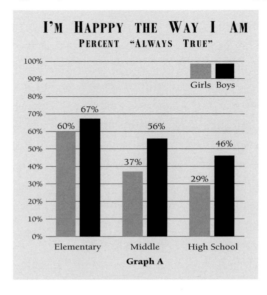

**I'M HAPPPY THE WAY I AM**
**PERCENT "ALWAYS TRUE"**

Girls Boys

Elementary: 60% Girls, 67% Boys
Middle: 37% Girls, 56% Boys
High School: 29% Girls, 46% Boys

**Graph A**

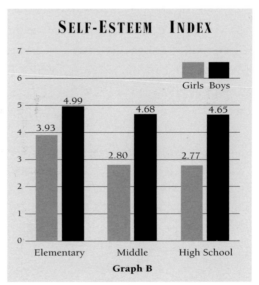

**SELF-ESTEEM INDEX**

Girls Boys

Elementary: 3.93 Girls, 4.99 Boys
Middle: 2.80 Girls, 4.68 Boys
High School: 2.77 Girls, 4.65 Boys

**Graph B**

## Declining self-esteem, a governor on dreams and future actions, more strongly affects girls than it does boys.

The overall declines in self-esteem during adolescence have their greatest impact on girls as self-esteem turns to action. The survey finds that adolescent girls are more likely than boys to have their declining sense of themselves inhibit their actions and abilities. This difference between girls and boys grows more pronounced with age.

The biggest difference in self-esteem between girls and boys centers on the subject of "doing things." Boys are much more likely than are girls to feel "pretty good at a lot of things." Almost half the boys say this statement is always true, compared to less than a third of the girls. Boys' sense of confidence in their ability to "do things" correlates strongly with general self-confidence.

Boys also report a greater willingness to speak out. Boys are more likely than are girls to "speak up in class a lot" and, as Graph C shows, to "argue with my teachers when I think I'm right."

As adolescent girls and boys get older, their confidence in their abilities reflects a growing gender gap. As Graph D shows, the 10 percentage point difference between elementary school girls and boys becomes a 19-point difference between high school girls and boys.

The greater sense of self-

**Adolescent girls are more likely than boys to have their declining sense of themselves inhibit their actions and abilities. This difference grows more pronounced with age.**

esteem among boys is apparent in their greater confidence in their own talents, a point of intersection between feeling and action. Almost twice as many boys as girls refer to their talents as what they like most about themselves. Boys' confidence in their ability in sports—four times as high for adolescent boys as for girls—is the source of much of the difference.

Physical appearance, fundamental to the self-esteem of all young people, is much more important to the self-image of girls than of boys. Girls are nearly twice as likely as boys to mention a physical characteristic as the thing they like most about themselves. Physical appearance is most important for girls in middle school, the time of greatest decline in self-esteem.

As girls and boys go through adolescence, both experience traumatic physical changes, and their perceptions of those changes are central to patterns of self-esteem. However, the way girls and boys see those changes and the degree to which those changes influence self-image differ sharply by gender. Boys tend to view the physical changes positively, as getting bigger and stronger. Girls believe their changes lead in a negative direction, reinforcing their declining self-esteem and gender stereotypes. Further, boys' greater confidence in their talents and their ability to do things cushions their uneasiness about changes in their appearance; in contrast, society tells girls more strongly that their worth is dependent on their appearance.

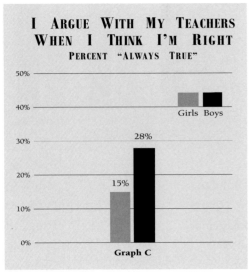

I ARGUE WITH MY TEACHERS WHEN I THINK I'M RIGHT
PERCENT "ALWAYS TRUE"

Girls  Boys

28%

15%

Graph C

Finally, self-esteem is critically related to young people's dreams and successes. The higher self-esteem of adolescent boys translates into bigger career dreams. Boys start out at a higher level than do girls when it comes to their career aspirations. The number of boys who aspire to glamorous occupations (rock star, sports star) is greater than that of girls at every stage of adolescence, creating a kind of "glamour gap." Further, boys are slightly more likely than are girls to believe their own career dreams will come true.

Finding it difficult to dream and feeling constrained by gender rules, girls start out with lower hopes for their careers, and are already less confident in their talents and abilities. Girls are much more likely than boys to say they are "not smart enough" or "not good enough" for their dream careers.

There are important interactions between race and trends in self-esteem. Black girls express high levels of self-esteem from elementary school through high school. While family and community reinforcement sustain high levels of personal importance for black girls, these girls feel strong pressure from the school system and experience a significant drop in positive feelings about their teachers and their schoolwork.

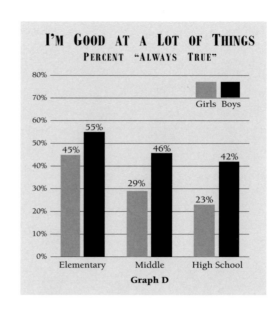

I'M GOOD AT A LOT OF THINGS
PERCENT "ALWAYS TRUE"

Girls   Boys

Elementary: 45% / 55%
Middle: 29% / 46%
High School: 23% / 42%

Graph D

Hispanic girls are much less confident and positive than black girls and go through a crisis in some ways even more profound than that of white girls. While Hispanic girls start with significantly higher levels of self-esteem than white girls, their confidence plummets in their appearance, family relationships, school ability, talents, and importance. Between elementary school and high school, their personal self-esteem drops 38 points, more than the drop for any other group of girls.

## Family and school, not peers, have the greatest impact on adolescents' self-esteem and aspirations.

Popular literature suggests that peers dominate the world of teenagers. In fact, the survey finds that several other factors, especially adults and the adult institutions of family and school, have a greater impact on adolescents' self-esteem and aspirations.

A factor analysis probe of self-esteem shows that a feeling of acceptance by peers ranks well below academic confidence and a feeling of importance within the family as a dimension of adolescent self-image.*

|  | Elem. | Middle | H.S. | Change | All |
|---|---|---|---|---|---|
| Girls' Self-Esteem by Race and Grade "Happy the Way I Am" Percent Always True | | | | | |
| White Girls | 55 | 29 | 22 | -33 | 34 |
| Black Girls | 65 | 59 | 58 | -7 | 60 |
| Hispanic Girls | 68 | 54 | 30 | -38 | 52 |

*Factor analysis is a statistical technique that looks at the underlying dimensions in attitudes across a number of questions, and at the relationships and relative importance of those dimensions.

Pride in schoolwork and a feeling of being good at things decline rapidly during adolescence. In elementary school, about half of the students always feel "proud of the work I do." By high school, only one in six students still feels that way.

Although the overall structure of self-esteem is similar for girls and boys, small differences provide important insights. For boys, the sense of confidence in their ability to do things correlates more strongly with general self-esteem than with other aspects of academic confidence. As they discover that people believe males can do things, adolescent boys gain self-esteem. According to the focus groups, girls find that people, including their teachers, believe girls cannot do the things girls think they can. The result for girls is lower self-esteem.

For girls, feelings about academic performance correlate strongly with relationships with teachers. Teachers are important role models for girls. Nearly three out of four elementary school girls and more than half of high school girls want to be teachers. Far fewer adolescent boys, at any grade, want to be teachers.

Thus, teachers have a special opportunity to affect the self-esteem of their female students, and, by instilling confidence, to shape their interests and aspirations.

For elementary school girls, in fact, academic self-esteem is the most important aspect of self-esteem; yet, it is for them already a negative force. Fewer than half the girls in elementary school (49 percent) say they feel pride in their schoolwork, and that percentage drops 32 points to 17 percent in high school. (The percentage of boys who are proud of their schoolwork also drops between elementary and high school, from 53 percent to 16 percent—but academic pride plays a much smaller role in the structure of boys' self-esteem.)

## How students come to regard math and science differs by gender.

One of the most dramatic and easily measured effects of schools and teachers on their adolescent students is in the teaching of mathematics and science. The survey finds a strong relationship between perceived math and science skills and adolescent self-esteem. Of all the study's indicators, girls' perceptions of their ability in math and science had the strongest relationship to their self-esteem; as girls "learn" that they are not good at these subjects, their sense of self-worth and aspirations for themselves deteriorate.

As Graphs E and F show, an overwhelming majority of young people like math and science. Most elementary school students also have confidence in their abil-

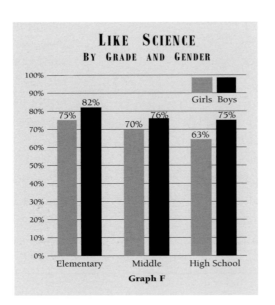

ity to do math, though levels are higher for boys than for girls. All students' enthusiasm for math and science is greatest in the elementary years and drops precipitously as they get older. Graph E shows the most dramatic losses are among girls.

- 81 percent of elementary school girls like math. By high school, 61 percent say they like math.

- 84 percent of elementary school boys like math. By high school this percentage drops too, but less than it does for girls, to 72 percent.

- Pluralities of elementary school girls (24 percent) and boys (32 percent) name math as their favorite subject. By high school, these percentages decline to 12 percent and 23 percent.

- Conversely, the percentage of girls who name math as their least favorite subject jumps from 15 percent in elementary school to 28 percent in high school. The percentage of boys who like math least jumps from 9 percent to 21 percent.

Although overwhelming numbers of adolescents "like" math, significantly fewer believe they are "good at math." As Graphs G and H show, adolescents' confidence in their ability declines as they get older and helps erode their enjoyment of math. Adolescent boys, at all grade levels, are much more confident than young girls about their abilities in math. Half of all elementary school boys, but only one-third of all elementary school girls, say they are good at math. By high school, one in four males, but only one in seven females, still says that he or she is good at math.

Adolescent girls and boys interpret their problems with math differently. Large percentages of both girls and boys who dislike math do so because they get bad grades or consider it too hard. As girls get older, the percentage who dislike math because it is "too hard" drops and the percentage who dislike math because they get "bad grades" increases. As the boys get older, they come to believe that they do not like math because the subject itself is "not useful." Girls interpret their problems with math as personal failures. Boys project difficulty more as a problem with the subject matter itself.

Interest in science shows similar patterns.

- The number of girls who like science drops from 75 percent in elementary school to 63 percent in high school.

- In elementary school 82 percent of boys like science; 75 percent of boys still like science in high school.

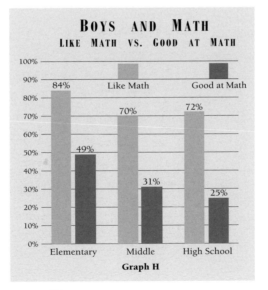

**GIRLS AND MATH**
LIKE MATH VS. GOOD AT MATH

Like Math    Good at Math

81%    68%    61%
31%    18%    15%

Elementary    Middle    High School
**Graph G**

**BOYS AND MATH**
LIKE MATH VS. GOOD AT MATH

Like Math    Good at Math

84%    70%    72%
49%    31%    25%

Elementary    Middle    High School
**Graph H**

While most students who dislike math do so because they consider it "too hard," most students who dislike science say science is "not interesting." However, as girls grow older, we see a similar pattern to that we saw with math. Adolescent girls are more likely than adolescent boys to find science uninteresting. Adolescent boys are more likely than girls to discount the importance of science itself.

## There is a circular relationship between liking math and science, enjoying self-esteem, and identifying career interests.

The school system provides the most important place to make a positive impact on the self-esteem of adolescents, as well as on their career preferences. The relationships between math and science, self-esteem, and career preferences provide an important example of the kind of difference schools can make. Because of the differences in the ways adolescent girls and boys think about math and science, the influence of teachers on young women and their self-esteem and careers is particularly strong.

Adolescents who say they like math and science are more likely to prefer careers in occupations that they believe make use of these subjects. By small margins, students who like math and science express stronger desires for careers as teachers, doctors, and scientists.

Even more important, students who like math and science are more likely to as-

**There is a circular relationship between enjoyment of math and science and self-esteem. Students who like math and science possess significantly greater self-esteem; students with higher self-esteem like math and science more.**

pire to careers as professionals. On an open-ended measure of career preference ("What do you really want to be when you grow up?"), students who like math and science are more likely to name professional occupations as their first career choice. The impact is stronger for girls than for boys.

Enjoyment of math and science is also related to career choice in a more indirect way. As Graph I shows, there is a circular relationship between enjoyment of these subjects and self-esteem. Students who like math and science possess significantly greater self-esteem; students with higher self-esteem like math and science more. These students like themselves more, feel better about their schoolwork and grades, consider themselves more important, and feel better about their family relationships.

The differences by gender are important. Dramatically, adolescent girls who like math are more confident about their appearance than are all adolescent boys, whether or not they like math (and than adolescent girls who do not like math). And girls who like math and science worry less about others liking them.

This greater sense of self-confidence has a measurable effect on confidence about career choices for both girls and boys. Girls and boys who like math hold onto their career dreams more stubbornly and are less likely to believe they will "probably end up being something different from what you sometimes want to be."

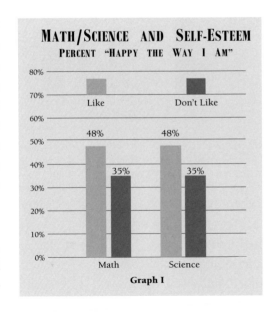

**MATH/SCIENCE AND SELF-ESTEEM**
**PERCENT "HAPPY THE WAY I AM"**

Like — 48% Math, 48% Science
Don't Like — 35% Math, 35% Science

**Graph I**

Finally, all adolescents see large differences between the sexes, and these differences increase the tensions and contradictions for girls as they get older. Gender stereotypes are still a major force in shaping the career expectations of young people. Girls are much more likely than boys to want to be homemakers (+32 percent), teachers (+33 percent), and nurses (+35 percent). Adolescent boys are much more likely to want to be sports stars (+42 percent), construction workers (+18 percent), and scientists (+21 percent). The work force in the year 2000 will require many more scientists, engineers, and mathematicians. However, by high school, while 52 percent of boys think they would enjoy being scientists, only 29 percent of girls share that opinion.

**The work force in the year 2000 will require many more scientists, engineers, and mathematicians. However, by high school, while 52 percent of boys think they would enjoy being scientists, only 29 percent of girls share that opinion.**

Still, the survey also reflects the dramatic societal changes in the last two decades. Most young people assume that women will combine a job outside the home with their job inside the home. Even more girls than boys think they could enter certain professions, most noticeably, the law.

These changes in gender perception are among the brightest findings of the survey, and signal a broad potential for even greater changes with a better understanding of the reciprocal relationships between schools and female students. These results present a critical challenge to schools as we face the social and economic realities of the next century.

*–Greenberg-Lake:*
*The Analysis Group*

# Afterword: Effecting Change

Never before has there been so much concern with improving American schools. And never before has there been so pressing a need for change to meet the educational needs of American girls, as well as boys.

As we prepare for a new century in which women will account for almost half of our work force, we must face facts: For America to have a first-class work force tomorrow, we must provide a first-class education for girls today. For U.S. students to rank first in the world in mathematics and science by the year 2000, we must reverse the notion that "girls aren't good at math and science."

Schools must play a role in changing the messages girls receive within their classroom walls. Despite popular beliefs that peer groups and peer pressure dominate the actions, values, and goals of teenagers, *Shortchanging Girls, Shortchanging America* shows that school and family have a greater impact on adolescents, especially girls.

## How Schools Set Girls Up to Fail

Schools transmit gender bias in the thousand and one signals they send girls and boys about what's expected of them. These expectations determine how girls and boys are treated, how they're taught, and ultimately how they're tracked onto different paths through their schooling and into their careers. In dozens of separate studies, researchers have found that girls receive less attention, less praise, less effective feedback, and less detailed instruction from teachers than do boys. Research

**For U.S. students to rank first in the world in mathematics and science by the year 2000, we must reverse the notion that "girls aren't good at math and science."**

by Myra and David Sadker, professors of education at American University, reveals:

- Teachers typically initiate more communication with boys than with girls in the classroom, strengthening boys' sense of importance.

- Teachers tend to ask boys more complex, abstract, and open-ended questions, providing better opportunities for active learning.

- In class projects and assignments, teachers are more likely to give detailed instructions to boys, and more likely to take over and finish the task for girls, depriving them of active learning.

- Teachers tend to praise boys more often than girls for the intellectual content and quality of their work. They praise girls more often for neatness and form.

- When boys perform poorly, teachers often blame failure on lack of effort. Girls receive a different message; the implication is that effort would not improve their results.

- All too often, teachers and counselors track girls away from courses of study that lead to high-skilled, high-paying, high-technology careers.

The barrage of negative messages hits girls at an especially vulnerable stage in their lives. As *Shortchanging Girls, Shortchanging America* shows, many of the same negative signals impact girls across racial and ethnic lines, though to somewhat varying degrees. New AAUW research will explore these variations further.

Of additional concern is how well prevalent teaching methods satisfy the individual learning styles of girls *and* boys. Some children, including many girls, learn better in cooperative settings. Competitive learning, favored in most classrooms, is a style that often puts girls at a disadvantage.

## Reinventing the Classroom

AAUW believes that teachers are spearheading an effort to bring needed change to the classroom. Increasingly, committed teachers are scrutinizing their teaching styles and classroom behaviors for the hidden messages they convey. The concept has gained so much credence that training on gender issues has been incorporated into some professional development courses for teachers.

Through its Eleanor Roosevelt Fund Teacher Fellowships, the AAUW Educational Foundation promotes the professional development of teachers in public school grades K–12. Each year selected fellows study ways to improve the teaching of math and science to girls in their classrooms. Fellows convene at an annual Teachers Institute to exchange ideas and experiences. Back in their home schools, they implement new teaching strategies and share them with their colleagues.

Some of these strategies are enjoying ever-wider circulation. To assure fairness in calling on students, former Teacher Fellow Alice Bowen, now an acting assistant

**AAUW believes that teachers are spearheading an effort to bring needed change to the classroom. Increasingly, committed teachers are scrutinizing their teaching styles and classroom behaviors for the hidden messages they convey.**

principal at the Burncoat Middle School in Worcester, Mass., uses flash cards with students' names on them. "I shuffle the cards and call the names randomly. It drives the kids crazy. They never know when their name is coming." Neither does she.

## Promoting Community Involvement

Parents, activists, and community leaders have gotten in the act, too. Following the suggestions of AAUW, parents are contacting the Title IX coordinators in their school districts to assess Title IX compliance in local schools. (Title IX of the 1972 Education Amendments is the federal law that prohibits sex discrimination in federally funded educational institutions.) Parents are also working with teachers and students to draft sexual harassment policies in schools.

Through coalitions with local businesses and community groups, parents and activists are exploring new programs to enhance girls' self-esteem. Collaborations with colleges and universities have also been productive. An AAUW brochure, "10 Tips to Build Gender-Fair Schools," describes other courses of action to effect change. (To request a free copy, call 800/326-AAUW, ext. 120.)

Parents, activists, and community groups who want to promote hands-on science, math, and technology activities for girls now have access to some excellent resources, such as the "Operation SMART" activity and planning guides published by Girls Incorporated in New York City. Projects in the book are designed specifically to interest girls ages 10 to 14, with text and photos reflecting that focus.

Civic and educational leaders from Philadelphia to Los Angeles will be able to draw from models of school gender-equity projects, funded by the AAUW Educational Foundation through a grant from the W.K. Kellogg Foundation. Community-based projects in the "Girls Can!" program reflect a variety of educational approaches, cultures, races, and ethnicities.

For information about the "Girls Can!" program or a list of the participating communities, call 202/785-7713. A short video about ways to correct gender bias in schools will be available in fall 1994 through AAUW. (For information on ordering, see page 18.)

AAUW has worked in coalition with groups like the National Education Association, the National School Boards Association, and the American Association of Colleges for Teacher Education to develop programs to promote change. These groups and others now incorporate gender equity goals in their own internal priorities.

## Girls in Mathematics and Science

Nowhere are the links between expectation and accomplishment clearer than in how girls and boys relate to mathematics and science. The AAUW survey found a crucial—and circular—relationship between self-esteem levels, interest in mathematics and science, and career aspirations:

- Girls and boys who like mathematics and science have higher levels of self-esteem. And girls and boys with higher levels of self-esteem like math and science.

> AAUW has worked in coalition with groups like the National Education Association, the National School Boards Association, and the American Association of Colleges for Teacher Education to develop programs to promote change.

- Girls and boys who like math and science are more likely to aspire to careers in which these subjects are essential.

- Girls and boys who like math and science are more likely to aspire to careers as professionals. This relationship is even stronger for girls than for boys.

- Girls who like math are more confident about their appearance and worry less about others liking them.

- Girls and boys who like math and science hold onto their career dreams more stubbornly. They are less likely to believe that they will be something different from what they want to be.

- Many more girls than boys lose interest in mathematics and science after elementary school.

Here again, progress is being made. AAUW community action grants have funded a number of math/science summer camps for girls. Chris Short, project director of a camp for eighth- through 10th-grade girls organized by the Lassen County, California, Branch of AAUW, says, "The young women walked away with strengthened self-esteem…They indicated on the camp evaluations that 'I am okay,' and 'I can do anything I want.'"

Similarly, teacher fellowships sponsored by the AAUW Educational Foundation's Eleanor Roosevelt Fund focus on developing new ways to draw girls into math and science. Former Teacher Fellow Betsy Adams, who teaches math at Jordan High School in Long Beach, California, sees these methods work. "Many girls begin my class with a negative attitude about math," she says. "By year's end, they believe they too can be math whizzes."

Policy recommendations in *The AAUW Report: How Schools Shortchange Girls* address other actions needed by educational, business, and political leaders to encourage the participation of girls in math and science.

## A Call to Action

It's time to commit ourselves to a school system and a society that encourage girls to attain their full potential. We in AAUW are doing our part.

By speaking out and commissioning credible research, we have led the fight for gender equity in our nation's schools. Our Educational Foundation published the first comprehensive study of research in the field: *The AAUW Report: How Schools Shortchange Girls*. The *Report*, which synthesized more than 1,300 published studies, documents the unequal treatment of girls in our nation's schools.

When *Report* data showed a higher than expected level of complaints about sexual harassment, the Foundation commissioned Louis Harris and Associates to conduct a new study. *Hostile Hallways: The AAUW Survey on Sexual Harassment in America's Schools* showed that four out of five students have experienced some form of sexual harassment in school, and

**"Many girls begin my class with a negative attitude about math," says former Teacher Fellow Betsy Adams, who teaches math at Jordan High School in Long Beach, California. "By year's end, they believe they too can be math whizzes."**

that girls suffer greater effects than boys. AAUW has also commissioned several new studies to identify educational strategies that work for girls.

We have convened roundtables with community, state, and national leaders to address gender equity needs. We have played a key role in the drafting of gender equity legislation now before Congress. We have provided leadership to the diverse community projects nationwide that are trying to provide encouragement to girls. And the Foundation's Eleanor Roosevelt Fund for Women and Girls has also awarded an average of 22 Teacher Fellowships a year for female K–12 public school teachers who are committed to finding better teaching methods to motivate girls.

But we cannot do it alone. Our work has been a catalyst for the changes that are needed in our educational system and in every other institution that influences the aspirations and achievements of our girls and young women.

The challenge is clear for all of us— parents and educators as well as leaders in business, government, and the media. Now is the time to think, speak out, and take action to help American girls be the best they can be. For when we shortchange girls, we shortchange America.

–July 1994

# Resources: The AAUW Equity Library

■

## Ground-breaking Works on Gender Bias in Education

**Schoolgirls: Young Women, Self-Esteem, and the Confidence Gap (Doubleday, 1994)**
Riveting book by journalist Peggy Orenstein in association with AAUW shows how girls in two racially and economically diverse California schools suffer the painful plunge in self-esteem documented in *Shortchanging Girls, Shortchanging America*. 384 pages. $18.95 AAUW members/$21.95 nonmembers.

**Hostile Hallways: The AAUW Survey on Sexual Harassment in America's Schools**
The first national study of sexual harassment in school, based on the experiences of 1,632 students in grades 8 through 11. Gender and ethnic/racial (African American, Hispanic, and white) data breakdowns included. Commissioned by the AAUW Educational Foundation and conducted by Louis Harris and Associates. 28 pages/1993. $8.95 AAUW members/ $11.95 nonmembers.

**The AAUW Report: How Schools Shortchange Girls**
Disturbing report documents girls' second-class treatment in America's schools, grades K–12. The research report, commissioned by the AAUW Educational Foundation and prepared by the Wellesley College Center for Research on Women, includes policy recommendations and strategies for change. 128 pages/1992. $14.95 AAUW members/$16.95 nonmembers.

**The AAUW Report Executive Summary**
Overview of **The AAUW Report** research, with recommendations for educators and policymakers. 8 pages/1992. $6.95 AAUW members/$8.95 nonmembers.

**The AAUW Report Action Guide**
Strategies for combating gender bias in school, based on **The AAUW Report** recommendations. 8 pages/1992. $6.95 AAUW members/$8.95 nonmembers.

**Action Alert**
AAUW's monthly newsletter monitoring congressional action on educational equity as well as reproductive choice, sexual harassment, and other vital issues. One-year subscription: $20 AAUW members/$25 nonmembers.

**Shortchanging Girls, Shortchanging America**
Highly readable executive summary of the 1991 poll that awakened the nation to the problem of gender bias in America's schools. Poll shows graphically how classroom gender bias hurts girls' self-esteem, school achievement, and career aspirations. Revised edition, with updated account of poll's impact and review of school, community, and government action strategies, highlights survey results with charts and graphs. 20 pages/1994. $8.95 AAUW members/$11.95 nonmembers.

**Full Data Report: Shortchanging Girls, Shortchanging America**
Complete data on AAUW's 1991 national poll on girls and self-esteem, with survey questions and responses, and banners displaying cross-tabulations. Includes floppy disk with all data. 500 pages/1991. $60 AAUW members/$85 nonmembers. *To order, call 202/785-7761.*

**Video: Shortchanging Girls, Shortchanging America**
A dramatic look at the inequities girls face in school. Features education experts and public policy leaders, AAUW poll results, as well as the compelling voices and faces of American girls. VHS format/15 minutes/1991. $19.95 AAUW members/ $24.95 nonmembers.

**Video: Girls Can! New Release: Fall 1994**
Profiles programs around the country that are making a difference in fighting gender bias in schools. VHS format. $19.95 AAUW members/$24.95 nonmembers.

**AAUW Issue Briefs**
Package of five briefs, with strategies for change: Equitable Treatment of Girls and Boys in the Classroom; Restructuring Education; Stalled Agenda—Gender Equity and the Training of Educators; College Admission Tests: Opportunities or Roadblocks?; Creating a Gender-Fair Multicultural Curriculum. 1990-93. $7.95 AAUW members/$9.95 nonmembers.

---

## Help Make a Difference for Today's Girls...and Tomorrow's Leaders

Become part of the American Association of University Women, representing 150,000 college graduates, and help promote education and equity for women and girls. You can add your voice as a Member-at-Large or work on critical issues in one of AAUW's 1,750 local branches. For further membership information, write: AAUW Membership, Dept. T, 1111 Sixteenth Street N.W., Washington, DC 20036-4873.

The AAUW Educational Foundation, a not-for-profit 501(c)(3) organization, provides funds to advance education, research, and self-development for women, and to foster equity and positive societal change. Your dollars support research, community action projects, fellowships for women, and teachers. Send contributions to: AAUW Educational Foundation, Dept. 294, 1111 Sixteenth Street N.W., Washington, DC 20036-4873.

# AAUW Resources Order Form

Name _____

Address _____

City/State/Zip _____

Daytime phone _____ AAUW membership # (if applicable) _____

| Item | Circle Price Member/Nonmember | Quantity | Total |
|---|---|---|---|
| **Schoolgirls** | $18.95/$21.95 | _____ | _____ |
| **Hostile Hallways** | $8.95/$11.95 | _____ | _____ |
| **The AAUW Report** | $14.95/$16.95 | _____ | _____ |
| **AAUW Report Summary** | $6.95/$8.95 | _____ | _____ |
| **AAUW Report Action Guide** | $6.95/$8.95 | _____ | _____ |
| **Action Alert** | $20/$25 per year | _____ | _____ |
| **Shortchanging Girls: Summary** | $8.95/$11.95 | _____ | _____ |
| **Shortchanging Girls: Video** | $19.95/$24.95 | _____ | _____ |
| **Girls Can!: Video** | $19.95/$24.95 | _____ | _____ |
| **AAUW Issue Briefs 5-Pack** | $7.95/$9.95 | _____ | _____ |
| | | **Subtotal:** | _____ |
| | | 6% sales tax (DC, FL residents only) | _____ |
| | | **Shipping/Handling:** | $4.00 |
| | | | _____ |
| **AAUW Membership** | $35 | _____ | _____ |
| | | **Total Order:** | _____ |

*For bulk pricing on orders of 10 or more, call 800/225-9998, ext. 294.*

**Please make check or money order payable to AAUW. Do not send cash.**

**Credit cards are accepted for orders of $10 or more.**

☐ MasterCard   ☐ Visa   Card #__ __ __ __ - __ __ __ __ - __ __ __ __ - __ __ __ __   Expiration _____

Name on card _____ Cardholder signature _____

**SATISFACTION GUARANTEED: If you are not completely satisfied with your purchase, please return it within 90 days for exchange, credit, or refund. Videos are returnable only if defective, and for replacement only.**

☐ Please send me information on joining an AAUW branch in my area (dues vary by branch).

☐ I'd like to join as a Member-at-Large. Enclosed is $35. (Fill in education information below.)

_____

College/University                    State/Campus                    Year/Degree

**FOR MAIL ORDERS, SEND THIS FORM TO:**
AAUW Sales Office
Dept. 294
P.O. Box 251
Annapolis Junction, MD 20701-0251

**FOR TELEPHONE ORDERS, CALL:**
800/225-9998, ext. 294

CODE: D95ROS

## Date Due

| | | |
|---|---|---|
| APR 0 9 2001 | | |
| 2/23/02 | | |
| OC 21 '03 | | |
| AP 7 '04 | | |
| AP 13 '06 | | |
| AUG 31 2009 | | |
| | | |
| | | |
| | | |
| | | |
| | | |
| | | |
| | | |
| | | |